LONG LIVE MAN

by GREGORY CORSO

LONG LIVE MAN

GREGORY CORSO

A NEW DIRECTIONS PAPERBOOK

Certain of these poems have previously appeared in the
following publications to whom grateful acknowledgment
is here made: *Between Worlds, Big Table, Evergreen
Review, New Departures, New Directions 17, Three
Arts Quarterly* and *Two Cities.*

Manufactured in the United States of America
New Directions books are printed on acid-free paper.

Published simultaneously in Canada by Penguin Books Canada Limited

New Directions Books are published for James Laughlin
by New Directions Publishing Corporation,
80 Eighth Avenue, New York 10011

Tenth Printing

to my father

1959-60

MAN

Prologue to what was to be a long long poem

The good scope of him is history, old and ironic;
Not modern history, unfulfilled and blurred —
Bleak damp fierce thunderous lightning days;
Poor caveman, so scared of the outside,
So afeared of its power and beauty,
Created a limit, and called that limit God —
Cell, fish, apeman, Adam;
How was the first man born?
And why has he ceased being born that way?

Air his fuel, will his engine, legs his wheels,
Eyes the steer, ears the alert;
He could not fly, but now he does —
The nails hair teeth bones blood
All in communion with the flesh;
The heart that feels all things in life
And lastly feels in death;
The hands in looks and action are masterful;
The eyes the eyes;
The penis is a magic wand,
The womb greater than Spring —

I do not know if he be Adam's heir
Or kin to ape,
No man knows; what a good driving mystery —
I can imagine a soul, the soul leaving the body,
The body feeding death, death simply a hygiene;
I can wonder the world the factory of the soul,
The soul putting on a body like a workman's coveralls,
Building, unbuilding, rebuilding.
That man can *think* soul is a great strange wonderful thing —

In the beginning was the word; man has spoken —
The Jews, the Greeks; chaos groping behind;
Exalted dignity sings; the blind angel's cithara
Twanged no chain-reaction that World War be the Trojan War,
Not with the goddess Eris denied a wedding seat;
No praise of man in my war, wars have lost their legendariness —
The Bible sings man in all his glory;
Great Jew, man is hard stem of you,
Was you first spoke love, O noble survivor;
The Greeks are gone, the Egyptians have all but vanished;
Your testament yet holds —

The fall of man stands a lie before Beethoven,
A truth before Hitler —
Man is the victory of life,
And Christ be the victory of man —
King of the universe is man, creator of gods;
He knows no thing other than himself
And he knows himself the best he can;
He exists as a being of nature
And sustains all things in being;
His dream can go beyond existence —
Greater the rose?
The simple bee does not think so;
When man sings birds humble into piety;
What history can the whale empire sing?
What genius ant dare break from anthood
As can man from manhood?
King Agamemnon! Mortal man!
Ah, immortality —

SUBURBIA MAD SONG

The horns are still
and marriage drops its quiet shoe.
How will the wife look at her husband
seated on a dark sofa, shy?
The best man is still drunk,
and the bridesmaid plucks her brummagem bouquet.
Gathered against the ants
a husband and wife calculate their worth;
they freeze tight on their chairs
troubled by the table
— He screams: "Housewife! Housewife!"
She screams: "Rinso white! Rinso bright!"
And when the child comes
he'll swoon unrelative to the dire of Elm Street.

DEAR GIRL

With people conformed
Away from pre-raphaelite furniture
With no promise but that of Japanese sparsity
I take up house
Ready to eat with you and sleep with you

But when the conquered spirit breaks free
And indicates a new light
Who'll take care of the cats?

ODE TO MYSELF & HER

Of self and non-self celebrate, lately mean —
       not your losing love; stay the gentle demon
       its lyrical fork jabs my strict skull
no evil conceals flesh under bone — You are not a mess
that you can never love again —
       once loved you know not what I distribute.

If there were a healthy night
       and blackness were perverse
       I should try the Venetian lamp's reflect:
The full-bodied Count who in water is skeleton
or just water, lost of reflection —
       But you grieve of an old night.

Of blackness decrepit, stocked with impossible shadows
       shades and sleeps — Stockclerk in the fact'ry of dream
       you freight silence from Death to all parts of life
you are all that I know
though a poor penmanship
       I know your hand.

On my council lap
       you burn the Arcadian map
       our only anthem'd direction
Now I can't tell in whose district you sit
nor can you boast in whose station I am
       blest with sweet melancholy.

When you unshacked the peachwolf from browngold air
       and I became received of bright perception
       It made no difference whether I believed you or not
We were but to break systems strike the circumference!
You to me and I to you
       you fulltime anatomy, I slightly humanized.

I pledged myself to misery you made beauty your seal
       Your song was the harmony of my song!
       Let us not compel hypocrisy
We so capable of great explosions!
I the dynamite you the igniter
       — No monster waltzes alone.

WHEN I THINK TO REFRAIN

The girls of the world and I
held tickets for food and sex

We watched Spring bypass Summer
letting Autumn in

Was then I decided to use
my final meal ticket

I had yet to use my sex ones

A hard girl admonished me
"This is not the behavior due us!"

THREE LOVES

1

Love.
It is a barren site in me now.
A pierced property with single ruin
— Me.
And though I'd the heart to traverse that vast acre
I'd only this inch of it, here, where I sit
Moaning: Memory prevail! Sweet sorrow hail!

She is here in absence;
Her absence be ever her presence
— Unlike the noble wrist waiting the dun hawk
I hold what has flown.

2

Oh if she'd only cease complaining things have altered!
"Nothing's the same!" she cries.
What good my telling her the oldest existing piece of huma
        writing
Begins with this sentence: "Things are not what they used to be.

The miserable girl kisses the cold rough wall
While I sit grieving hushed and heavy.
"So many are sick!" cries she;
"And the best are soon to be!"

3

And oh and now I know
Having had enough of her
How women suffer.

WALK

God how I love this walk!
Valleys depict the might of mountains
Hills swarm down with Mongols
Ledges wage smoke signals
Cliffs need lashing waves and English girls
Caves of hibernation and neolithic man
Dry endless wells
Pits of animal death
Grottos enshrined by holy visions
Gorges crevices the doomed adventurer falls in
Ghosts inhabit canyons also wild horses
Hapless mines
Cauldronous volcanoes
Sing! rock father of early earth
Orchestrate with granite baton
Sing gold sing crystal sing the fossil packed in you
Find song for the black knuckles of apeman
Stone! O beautiful stone
you are the coffin of dinosaurs
the pit of God's fruit — sing!
Ah but you difficult coal
you convict salt

BEYOND DELINQUENCY

What can the Deathmonger bring — horror delayed?
     Health's fooly alibi:
Life a trivial sacrament spitting eternity?
Persistence betrays yesterday's doubt, there is no more ugliness,
     nor ever was — What drills this compliment to Beauty?
Everyone is asleep, something like a cunning lullaby
     or a child's wreck dares — Fullness or failure,
     the allotment is perfect, Life, countenance of a drift
     a drowse, slow and sleep, a death, it cannot be Absolute.
There is sorrow in eternity, call it heaven,
     Life does not deny the affinity —
What can sold-out Death even bring? Repentance lifts
     its cheap despair,
It cannot see children pause before tired men
     with untimed eyes —
This is not the bravo definite, Oh so remote the sustenance!
How well I knew such sight—possessor of the hand to touch it too!
     Majesty with vast veins —

There is a gangwar which changes nothing,
     not all the stubborn reasons of youth
     can harbor at this stretched turn;
The Deather of the cub of the Royal Dukes perhaps knew
     the very rich meaninglessness of Life too;
Two-Thumb the holy terror from Red Hook
     broke his head with an unread book
     — chance to time their eyes
Life is many times accomplished, it cannot fail
     or be postponed;

The countless dying prompts more than Death
      — as in the distance
      The little light's approach becomes a train —

Heaven is sad, it is God who cries
      heavy like the seas — Not for Harlem or the Bronx
Nor something as old and forgotten
Hurtling the Acanthians against the Chalcidians
Here the Puerto Ricans of Life by no divine element
      but man's plastic sun
      outstand no history —
Pain is a sacred deliverance;
All that of Life can speed supreme, the angelical inpath
      in which hopeless delivery boys might
      pick and set their own hip elements
      as though the realm were a pasteboard —
Reason enough to hand them the sceptre
      and have them sit no less environed kings —

DEATH OF THE AMERICAN INDIAN'S GOD

The Mandan village is covered with snow
The blanketed chiefs on parfleches blow
Women in tufts of weasel press tapioca
And the lacrosse game is almost over —
Fling wompsikkucks at the Evening Star
The Mighty One Tirawa Atius is lain
      on the bright travois

He in His own raced hills and valleys
      wore skins birds and calumets
He in His own the laughing Koyemshi
      dogclowned all our sunsets
Give proper ceremony O Pawnee
The last caribou has been arrowed
      the last trout speared
Beetle bells and medicine yells
Everyone is dressed in crow

      They were the redmen
      feathers-in-their-head men
      now
      down among the dead men
      how

FIRST NIGHT ON THE ACROPOLIS

for Mr Martin, a Princeton professor of theoretical games

The night was right
All the plugs of heaven seemed in
The night was black was white
And the moon like a woman's breast
Nippled the Parthenon full

Quickly in and out the colonnade
Like a festering ghost
This is what was dreamed
And this were no dream
There the caryatids in moon shade
There the caryatids
The caryatids

Pressed face against a pillar I cried
Cried for my shadow that dear faithful sentry
Splashed across the world's loveliest floor

GREECE

They've reached the moon and I've reached Greece
and New York children are murdering each other
and breast promotion at worst yields ass-wine
so my goofiness is my goofiness and my drunk
worthy of insects trees and actions long since acted
I don't care about the Asiatics something I'll never obtain
and the fire I sleep can not reinstall — I still question
if all life is a rotary club and if it's death to resign —

Temporal on Acropolis I sit
amid hideous Stonepecker
listening to Athena's bitter remnants yellrake below —
What do I think now on this polis in this petrified snow?
My favorite statue is in England
the seated Demeter my dark learning electric chair —
And if that merciful lap would allow me sunset
I'd sit at sunset with no proclamation
but that of full savor nor asked of glory —
Stony madonna each strap an amorous privilege
your noseless mendicant now my days laughed out
where go the ground? A bird falls and cannot land —
Gods! ye ghastly syndicate down down
the golden the imminent palm over an age of sweet crime
downspread and favor mortal Zeus
what favor but that of continual immortality —
Ah don't look up kitten Olympian
immortality is neither up nor down
take your thousand year cargo
and twirl your mellowing crown
splash dustfate wealth oh dance ye bleak ancestry

frenzy your metric health away
the outrageous allotment roils
and futures can scarcely wait —
Poor gentle Greece — color of my sneakers —
I gem a sight not man or nature affords —
Dip your fingers Apollo churn light
the cycle is re-done — Look! the well-sighted
charioteer follows a slow stream —
The neo-Greek before the Tower of Winds
fingers his worrying beads and all his whims
craft and sodomy herald his proud virility
unlike those left in Sicily — black hands —
If the Maffia of Hermes is offensive
the beggars ought to heed that offense
nor scorn the blood engrossed by the offended —
The angels that men can never be also kill
Vengeance keeps brotherhood certain and remain'd —

In this my second night Athens
I walk with Pacific images of World War 2
Planes with sand-filled cockpits
Flame throwers laughing into pillboxes
Palm-wreathed snipers
Endless aloha cemeteries
— And the Parthenon is up there
Was there then
But "then" is gone
What was "then"?
Oh I'd the silver alphabet of the Sirens
the emptiless chimes crusted by centuries
the flying hyacinth cypress squadrons
Go away heavy chicken! With dream at interview we agreed
I'd the cracking gritty seraph —

Why did they take the caryatid away I asked
        the cameraman
The English The English he screamed —
When the crows of Acropolis like ants
brought Greece to their Queens — so did
the beep of worms bring air-rubies
to their soft blanket of human skin —

O isles! dry wartshells of Poseidon
Poseidon his thrice-pronged scepter is a barnacled bone
He no longer rides his frolicky sea-throne
He is flapping on the dry roof of the sun —
Far-off Samos that solitary isle of Victory
broke accustomed water with holy flee!
Oh it swam that lands join it more!
— Murdering as it stroked the idle oriental shore —
And thick arms length dragon Crete
in its sweetest saddest trek kinder than
wrinkled Circe dappling crap on her oinky lovers —
What worlds lovely Delos counterfeits!
Trophies of imagined cities could never trick into being —
Is that Poseidon running
flat on the bottom of the sea?
He's ten times the size of man
and though the waves break like fireworks
his long black beard is neatly flowed.

A God Greece never knew
mops the Periclean floor
At last some great event is due
Hear! Hermes is at the door
— who will take the message?

Hellene mothers cast off your rheums
Where is your golden child of the age?
Haste! else the Denier gather your wombs
A great god has entered the Hephaestion
ah there's the Hephaestus clumping to greet him
Zeus, the opposer of Zeus? The superior of Poseidon?
Quick ye mothers ere the merciful apparition dim —

Gymnasium of Diogenes lost in you
all made up like a scarecrow
a refugee from the grape festival
I am bleeding
having been stabbed ceremoniously by the Vine-Rat
I come to you weary of autumn harvest fairs
heavy with crackling chickens and crows —
Do I impersonate New York City?
Do I lie the East Side?
Is it for me to wipe my dirty pickle hands on the plektron?
        O greenless land once so green!
        St. Paul has chased your gods away
        and with them took your fertility
        — nor shall Demeter ever come back
Is this my song? Do I forget my New York City subway
        and rooftop sleep
But the sight of ecru-shredded Nike coiled in moonmarbled
        snow
her rippling gown her ever-loosened sandal seen
        in my 17th year
is more to me than the sight of the subways hurtling
against the rooftops or the sad meaning of Times Square
steaming into Central Park into the fat eyes
        of the napkined square

looking out on ducks, excusing the codes of day
touching no holy powers holding no word —
Bitter remnant Agora St. Pauled — a sick ruin
Though Theseus fleshmocks well
And napkined hallucinations may here too
sit with fat eyes and look out on ducks
I'd this my song — was here not New York City
white lions were on the roof
magnificent flowing manes fiery white
and they moved slowly circling me never looking at me
and I was not afraid I did not cry
I knew this life was more than visible
this brutal sphere speakable to heaven
thank God I have kind condenses dreamstream my scope
and so be roamed by white beasts
they take not part of me they do not see me
        chanceless command! what miracle to obey?
No alluring resemblance can claim such beauty!
Is this then the sly bond the surprise reward song affords —
Sweet Greece! though my dream of thee
is tremendous Greece, your credit is heavenly
I front the credulous —
The caryatid I am is Truth
Lo! my pediment of Lie —

Athens menu: Honey Figs Olives Grapes

Athens sky:
Like a magician's handkerchief blue becomes red
Earth's texture shreds
Aurora and amber grapple for dominancy —

Hydra, only isle of my touch & sight
where came where came that skinless light
Hydra, "thy beauty which did
haunt me in my
sleep to undertake
the death of all the
world" — This my first night I dreamed
we piled in the car
each with his cigarette of Death
I'd only one puff for its foul taste
they'd all of it for they wanted to die —
And woke once again to the meaning & meaninglessness
        of Life.
Life I love you
even though I am fifty miles ahead of you
I love you
even though my hands smell of death
how could I not love you
are you not the starting point of this
strange wondrous journey?
        I left your head and
entered your black hat
Oh the brilliant lining!
What is not there is present!
Many many are the occurrences of Light!
Overcreatures gazeless like grapes
Wondrous unbeasts blazing crests of undercreatures
Even one thin perched stony lion
Ball-bellied the color of the Rat!
Nor would it take part or look at me —
Hydra of Light! I left my earnings pile during the ray blessing
arrived with a cliché spiel of Death: a French car

screeching in my ear how *real* it was!
Behind the wheel Death, a big sloppy faggot;
He opened the door I *had* to get in!
For one whole year he sucked me off, and I always came!
But did not come to die.
In you Hydra I left this mistrustful light
spotted out almost died and entered a skinless light
I have acknowledged Death's good warrant and did flench
       much gold
I have rubbed heritage with reason and furtherment
balanced my dumb childhood to stir the can
wept away the goofs and hang-ups put down poetry
       as a coalminer's hat
and vowed to concern myself with deep seedlife not black
       candy —
I did not cry night hold the knife in day stay
When was it when was it — we piled in the car
each with his cigarette of Death . . .
Over and over I repeat:
Outstep the circle acknowledge Death's good warrant
and do not die
Step back in and know the universe goes one way
and you the other —
Truth why has man Frankensteined you
You are the *big lie* Truth
It is you who stops man from outstepping himself
In every man there is a lovely death but none shall die it
— Truth stands in the way.

Back in Athens he said: A friend of yours has died
I asked Who
He answered I don't remember

I screamed at Death I'm fed up with you! Stupid subject!
        Old button!
I unsalute you. On to greater things I go!
        — the soul's mechanic is done

And went to Agamemnon's brown dream where
I made treaties with industry and drank & married Fame
and led a German tourist girl into Clytemnestra's tomb
and in the morning ran from the pimple of reality on her face —
And went to Olympia where the sun streamed on Apollo's revery
a bright siege a gold rape
And Corinth where I wondered New York City leveled to the
        ground —

Hear me hear
        the once Grecian
Grecian no more
        charged with rusty minutest liberty
            kingdoms dust at her victory
I've new delight — and eternally toward delight
        I've a possession to assume
            to bestow

REFLECTION IN A GREEN ARENA

Where marble stood and fell
into an eternal landscape
I stand ephemeral

Anchored to a long season in a quick life
I am not wearied
nor feel the absence of former things
my relation to my country
the weak dreams   their weaker success
the reactions to death
and lovelessness

And oh and now I know
having had enough of her
how women suffer
And that hate which men bash against men
suffers less and is with end
but a woman's loss   endless
How I wish she were yet again
with all her solemnities

Ah good consoling Greece
She was not the love I know
Having crossed over into her world
I became the sad unlove
which separates us so

Poor America poor Russia
Thank God the moon has happened them
And France Algeria what sad geo-woe
Burnt peace as obstinate as nature
seems to be the ardor of history

I wipe the dead spider
off the statue's lips
Something there is is forgotten
and what's remembered slips
Butterfly and fly and other insectai
wait themselves to die

And so it's Spring again   so what
The leaves are leaves again   no tree forgot

HORSES

Joy to horses!
Horses by the sea are listening to me;
do you suppose they are listening to me,
breathing and heaving and neighing to me?
Horses of night are there;
horses of light and delight and nightmare,
they are there,
completely satisfied with the sea,
completely satisfied with me.

TO H.S.

Streets that crack because of blood;
Houses that are thatched with mud
— Long have I lived indoors
      by a picture window.

A bitch barks; the cobbles shine
      in the night
— I think of you, my angel friend,
Out there alone in all the world.

The schoolteacher is dead;
The chalk lies broken by the blackboard
— What more can you learn, gentle soul,
Out there alone in all the world?

How old the cakes on my table;
How thick the dust!
— I wait and wait, my friend;
The moon a wafer of Holy Communion
      on my window.

BY OSCAR WILDE'S GRAVE

While flies and bees Z in the argentry
       of this day's lipsome vestry
Oscar Wilde flees down the sphinx
       with the tailor's spatchcock and tormentil

Did Oscar infer
clothes made the man
see life and or death
       in the cravateur?

Aye was prison garb broke him
— denied a flower in his lapel

Take away a man's mask
and there'll be a cold sun
And there only the dead bask

Come now! Here was a man robust!
lost like a snow polar
       floating deathbound on an ice floe
doomed like the laughter of surging salmon
His house was a stone's throw from death

Gentility whispered repose
Twilight he populated
He'd no friend
only a problem
       and a rose

WRIT WHEN I FOUND OUT HIS WAS AN
UNMARKED GRAVE

Children children don't you know
Mozart has no where to go
This is so
Though graves be many
He hasn't any

LOVE DIRGE

Adorned with fragrant satyrians
      she glides assigned to green
      toward the breaking unisea
Up rises her lover
      dripping sparkling cartilage
September will call them to die
      lovely melocotones

HAPPENING ON A GERMAN TRAIN

From a fast-moving train window
on my way to King Ludwig's castle
I watched past a recurrence of trees
a white bird fly straight and low;
how extraordinary how it kept
up to the speed of the train
— then suddenly I heard two loud pops
resound in the sky;
the bird disappeared.
The train slowed to a stop
and everyone looked out the windows,
"There it is! There!"
Down at an angle
so smooth so sleek so silent
a white American jet fighter plane
CRASHBOOM and billows of orange.

*Note: The two pop sounds having been the release
of the ejector seat which parachuted the pilot to safety.*

EUROPEAN THOUGHTS — 1959

If there was never a home to go to
there was always a home not to go to
Well I know when a child as a runaway
I slept on the subway
and it would always stop
at the station where the home I ran from was
That was the bitterest sorrow oh it was

How would it be if I
ran up to every man I encountered
and with a big happy smile said:
"Isn't everything great!"
Or ran into a crowded restaurant and yelled:
"Bon appétit!"

When the ladies of Germany at war's end
stood amid the rubble wondering their men
and the old poked in the rubble for their homes again
did they not see the many-legged swastika
nudge like a bug under the rubble
pregnant with peace?
It seems German children were not spared
fifteen years later, today,
the sorrow of that rubble.
There are other things written on walls
Can Merde shock more than 卐 ?
And things like U S GO HOME
ALGERIA IS FRENCH or REMEMBER HUNGARY
are they really worse than MERDE?

And Greece was a marvelous country
but of course I was not marvelous in it
because man is made to suffer in a happy place
when he has been happy all too happy
in an insufferable place.

SAINT FRANCIS

Composed, to the series by Giotto, on a hill in Fiesole
overlooking Florence, Spring 1960

FRANCIS & THE BIRDS

I praise you your love,
Your benediction of animals and men,
When the night-horn blew,
And the world's property was disproportioned,
Where ere the winged children,
The rabbit,
The afterglow —
Good human tree, birds come to rest;
Not only those which chirp
But also those that honk and caw;
I see you with eagle,
Penguin, vulture, seagull;
Nor be it a bird
But an elephant, a herd!
All on your goodly compassionate shoulders.

FRANCIS & THE MIRACLE OF THE WATER

I'm thirsty for something,
something old and hard as rock;
and I don't doubt my thirst will be satiated —
Ab initio intro, Greek marble breasts
did ablactate me; how can I doubt
you'd the Bright Plumber's wand
to turn the old hard rock's faucet on —

SAINT FRANCIS HOLDING THE CHURCH
FROM FALLING

The Church is steadfast.
Computers pistons engines hydros dynamos museum it;
All is real estate.
What once gave light to dark
Now gives dark to light.
The Church should not fall
But walk away
And leave behind the glory of its stay —

What is Church?
A mink-necked eccelesiastic with problematical shouts?
Trinklet tabernacles with sacred and profane truths?
The morning high mass for a dead child in carnations?
The evening stillness of an old priest in prayer?
Church is quiet!
Even Lucifer, that once great rebel, is stilled.
St. Sebastian no longer stands full-bodied;
The arrows cling to bone.
I see Christ a skeleton on the cross.
If the Church falls and stone does fall,
If Church-idea is forgotten and ideas are forgotten,
I know within my soul that Christ will always be.
Nothing can erase that wonder of man;
Not bomb not anti-Christ nor thought nor me.
Christ is the victory of man
And so made your life, Francis, and most our history —

FULL LENGTH PORTRAIT OF SAINT FRANCIS

Francis, are you any stranger than Sitting Bull?
You are gone,
And gone the Andrews Sisters too.
What do I really know of you?
That you sent man forth naked
And yourself sent;
That you spun your lovers under sun to faint
And rise wherever and depart there;
That you made vacant by wish a pig's foot
And so wept the vacancy
And so blessed the vacanter —

Francis, I speak to you full:
What good that which is not dead and can do nothing
And with cunning complaints to life lives
And threatens to die and dies not?
What good the present that sets
Like a vaporous tent on the past
And sits within a beady prophet of future?
What good that neo-architect
Drenched in the pageant of roseate Babylon
Scheming crumbling cities to come?
I ask what good anything
If the death-law be enforced?
Death is not man's property
Yet man has raised a vast Hilton there —
What good the holy father holding his right hand over man
When man marries and breeds children
And at his Sunday table upholds the death-law?
What good what is blest by fortune and external harmony
When judgment makes up the middle
And carrion-things harbor the circle full?

What good what augments water so to give increase
      to water?
The fish that follows water is to the time of water;
More water makes not for more time —
What good a proper frame of mind on which foundations rest
When what is built thereon has no permanence?
What good the magnificent wonders of man
If man hurt another man?
What good armies if they are not painted ones?
What good mothers if they give birth
In spite of armies and death-law?
What good Hemingway if electric chair?
Francis, I am nearing thirty
And have not died as I romantically wished
And I am glad that I will be thirty
Because I find man indeed life's victory.
So hail every baby born by every mother
For each child is the second coming, yes!
Welcome new age! New space! New whatever!
I feel you near, I hear!
Future Exarchs and Viceroys and Savoies, hail!
Hail magnificent nudity!
I kiss you, little Lichtenstein!
Birth and millennium, Francis, Giotto,
Hail —

FRANCIS CHASING THE DEMONS OUT OF THE CITY

What good you Tritons and Nereids
with your tridents and sea-wreaths when there's Alcatraz?
What good you Statue of Liberty or Galatea,
the sea is hardly free,
Rikers Island, Ellis Island, Welfare Island;
there the demons, those sad mad structures,
where wardens, executioners, and guards feast;
it's not Mithras kills their eat,
nor the wine they drink be Bacchus kind —

I WHERE I STAND

for Alan Ansen

I where I stand   Venice
Aging my modern vision on winged lions
Impossible dreamer of cloaks and masks
Counting passion madrigals variegated figs
Where I stand   Venice   aging   counting

Peepholes in my Ducal Palace stay
I simply saw the proudest Doge
Superior favorable come to steal
Some wandering look from my eyes
I   where I stand

Blind as hags
Sometimes approaching black totality
        Knowledge of the dreamed city   lead the way
Although I am the very spot on which I stand

If when the infection of many years gone
Returns to me at death
I should see in final vision my ragged childhood
Leaning against bright alabaster walls
Munching strips of Euganean wheat
I will remain where I stand
And become timorous

Oh I should see it is fitting so
The mighty Doge   The winged lion
Princes and patriarchs   It is possible!
They while their carrion deeds in dream of me
I where I stand   Venice
The outskirts of a dreamed map

SURA

Pinch the air that its shriek might break silence.
Nature is done.
The Seasons have ended their alliance
And so the sun.

Twist the elf's knotty arm it must drawl thuds of joy.
Light must return
And reprieve the earth with its merciful stain.
— Fairy, tip the urn.

Think like a clock with no time to tell.
Hear the knell of your thoughts and wonder the bell.
Leave your sights of life nor comprehend fear
— Death is not anywhere near.

Hurry! Mountains are falling on valleys.
Trees are getting lost.
— Is this the one? Is that the one? Which tree was it?
I remember distinctly a *difference* among them.
Can I see one tree, know it well, and knowing, see all trees? —
Quick! Quick! Oceans are slipping into other oceans.
Fear not! Nothing can break your heart.
Life has it you make the Crack
And like the nail that meets the hammer
Depart.
Not the fly with your magnitude wonder why.
Yourself wonder but with silence and sly.
Watch you move from pot to pan — don't cry.

No thing can ever break your heart.
When your dreams are fullest the cruel hammer will blow
And die at your heart.

Too late! The sky is brown.

GOD? SHE'S BLACK

Gases and liquids Her nature
spewing stars like eggs
from Her All-Central Womb

Solids and solutions Her procedure
setting galaxies like babies
on Her All-Genetic Lap and Knee

Atoms and light Her law
punishing evolution like bad boys
with the slap of Her All-Void Hand

Metals and alloy Her chore
raising telescopes like puberty
toward Her All-Encompassed Self

Time and infinity Her Store
giving chance and speed like youth
— and all Her Sons leave home

Hydrogen and space Their war
creating bombs and rockets to what end?
Will They ever reach Her again?

GONE THE LAST DANGER ON EARTH

Great explosions of joy
Billows of clotted day
Running women sheets clotheslines
Mothers holding children
Children holding dolls
Earth's hornhigh hour
Nothing now nor man
What cries is gone
Universal good steps near
Path adorned
Excelsior veered
Divine bees suck the sun
The clear distillation of night into dawn

THOUGHT

Death is but is not lasting.
To pass a dead bird,
The notice of it is,
Yet walking on
Is gone.
The thought remains
And thought is all I know of death.

1961

EDEN WERE ELYSIUM

The stars like beaten grain are quell;
Throughout the universe the swipple is fell.

Regeneration; and that death
We all must die before we die;
And that death which became our birth,
Transeunt life, the dream, the real,
The blind of blue and yellow,
Birth + death = green;

Spring; the leaves are reborn,
The egg is precocial,
The transhumanence begins,
The cyclic apples blossom,
And snakes shed their skins.

NATURE'S GENTLEMAN

My first English fog!
And come at the right time too!
Had a terrible night
        in which I cursed gentlemanliness

So out into it I go
        and ho the detective's hollow walk
Mary Dare? Art thou Mary Dare?
And banged straight into a tree
and said: Excuse me

MR. MONEYBAG'S LAMENT

To have my earnings pile in the great ray;
to have not a cent drop off a beam;
to whist away the pit from the fruit,
surrounded by sweets, spice, and grenadine.
But I must abandon my earnings;
I've only one choice — giving.
I will and can unloose what I have earned,
even though my savings are nil.
I will never make treaties with industry.
Yet from it I did flench much gold
and thus my fortune
— now crashing down.
What can it mean this stockbond ribaldry?
Hanging for stealers, fat rugs, charity;
no need to juggle the books
— all wealth is come from the sad meaning of man.
Lock up the bright manufacturer, he knows
        but blank ambition.
It would be best to de-gangsterize merchantry;
Auction my come
        the sex-proprietor is bankrupt.
Murdock and dolphin heart will no longer be served.
Was I ever one to sue a seed for its apple?
Why then do they steal my kind progress?
What beady commerce now?

THE LOVE OF TWO SEASONS

When once in wildhood times
I'd aerial laughter my mischief

When once she opened her arms
And held me with excited tenderness

I laughed
She laughed

Our passions transcended
What in seriousness repelled us

And she bid me close my eyes
And behold some dreadful magnificence

Running ice
Cold pulse

Memories of iceday icenight
She told me goodbye forever

A month later
A no-return-address letter came

"I've a snow owl
And it loves you it loves you"

THE SENILE GENIUS

His mind is dead
and words, like so many worms,
      incorporate it.

He speaks what invokes a dark career;
chance, faith, a delusion;
a blind trek needs but one step
      to frustrate its end.

His is a fulsome imagination
doffed in wild confusion
— twilight,
      and thriceward is night.

Put him in the bin,
and woolly pigs be his allegorical calling.
Ceased cherished conveyance of good and cheer,
      all's wretched languor to attend.

My God but he's not *that* augean!
Scarcely a word uttered and wham!
      he finds himself up against
      some creep of a quaestor
      who'd have it water wash water.

Put him in the bin;
his outbursts are become nothing but
      prestigious flukes.
What good his snake oils
      his connubial remedies;
he's nothing apothecary.

Yet he's satisfied.
If the world should stop
      and a vast death strike,
he'd fold his life like a dollar,
      exact with care;
life be pure gain,
      and death no loss.

Something there is is not elsewhere
      but here;
the flagon's in a fell hand,
      and the mighty altongue's regardant.

Put him in the bin,
foolish to defend that brain;
swear some nascency there,
he's finished! done for!
      No more.

DEATH COMES AT PUBERTY

I touched that which generates terror in children,
I touched it, and was familiar with the touch of it,
Yes, I touched myself 31 years ago,
And beyond that, all was extra touches.
I touched to completion
That optimistic death which becomes a man.

FRIEND

Friends be kept
Friends be gained
And even friends lost be friends regained
He had no foes he made them all into *friends*
A friend will die for you
Acquaintances can never make friends
Some friends want to be everybody's friend
There are friends who take you away from friends
Friends believe in friendship with a vengeance!
Some friends always want to do you favors
Some always want to get NEAR you
You can't do this to me I'm your FRIEND
My friends said FDR
Let's be friends says the USSR
Old Scrooge knew a joy in a friendless Christmas
Leopold and Loeb planning in the night!
Et tu Brute
I have many friends yet sometimes I am nobody's friend
The majority of friends are male
Girls always prefer male friends
Friends know when you're troubled
It's what they crave for!
The bonds of friendship are not inseparable
Those who haven't any friends and want some are often creepy
Those who have friends and don't want them are doomed
Those who haven't any friends and don't want any are grand
Those who have friends and want them seem sadly human
Sometimes I scream Friends are bondage! A madness!
All a waste of INDIVIDUAL *time* —
Without friends life would be different not miserable
Does one need a friend in heaven —

HALLOWEEN

Children and many strangely things
wait their wings
watching yellow leaves and a red sun fall —
There goes Bunch Bunch haycocking
the Octob'rian argosy
he's a great bushel of apples
and now a black sky
now an orange sea —
Within Groot's twisted oaky gnarl
by a pumpkin's grinning glow
the wingmaker in chaste leprosy does sew
His owl suspects the broom
The mean cat as usual is scared out of its wits
and in a little dark corner
        trembles the entire room —

STARS

Central the hole of creation
Escape hatch from impending light
Uncreatures of space leap out
— Vivid fossils embedded in the night

THE THIN THIN LINE

How easy it is to go to sleep.
To be awake and then not awake.
Half-death, sawing the log Z,
Or sheep hurdle
— I sleep smarter these nights;
That is, I don't give in so easily.
I want to know what it is puts me out,
Click, out, just like that, Z,
Every night of my life.

You'd think I'd lose sleep
Lying awake like that
Waiting for the *click*.
Nay, I stayed up for two nights
Thus to make sure the third night
Would have me very tired. I was.
I lay on the bed, eyes opened,
Waiting the moment before Z,
That thin thin line
Between wake and sleep.

It began to happen.
I was falling asleep.
I was conscious of it.
I — but watching it like that
Kept me awake.
If I wanted to fall asleep
I had not to be conscious.
It was hard. It was very hard.

I was lying on the bed.
I was tired, awfully tired.
I knew I could easily fall asleep
If I didn't keep watch for it to happen.

I woke up
Ignorant of what put me to sleep.

UPON MY REFUSAL TO HERALD CUBA

Where does one stand who contends
a stand taken is a fall invited?
Nameless fear, I've long ago named you me;
I am not afraid of standing or falling;
there are countless positions to assume
to believe, to hold, to die for,
and some are worthy, just, purposeful —

Ever fast the world!
Best to tease all sides with awakening vibrations;
Cheerful remedies, calm or drastic solutions —

Of all that falls, of all that fell, of all to fall,
not Lucifer, not Adam, not Egypt,
but death and death alone is able
          to stand where it fell —

FIRST NIGHT IN THE WHITE HOUSE

The Potomac's sunset was wonderful
and the new President
after a long festive day
falls asleep on Lincoln's bed

He dreams jackdaws
And no matter how soft he nears
and his hand
no matter what the offering
— away they fly

TO DIE LAUGHING(?)

I came into the world
and laughed at what I saw
Indeed today is laughable
but beware such laughter

It can fill you with sorrow
It were best to contradict
Laugh at tomorrow
but keep today strict

Yet if I leave this world
and weep that I must leave
then indeed I am laughable
and nothing to believe

SEED JOURNEY

There they go
and where they stop
trees will grow

The nuts of amnesiac squirrels
more nuts will be
Bur takes freight on animal fur
And pollen the wind does carry

For some seeds
meal is the end of the journey

THE SAVING QUALITY

Bad nights of drunk
make bad days of sorry

Last night was stained with fear
I or the world was all wrong

Today in hard wind and rain
I stand on Putney's bridge
flinging Ritz crackers to the swans
ducks and gulls below
assuring myself:
        day or night
        you're all right

THE FAIRY TALE HERO

To the call of his country
he treks the length of years to face his king.
And the king, while others laugh, leans forward,
examines him, and with Godspeed
sends him forth to slay a beast not yet contrived.

The old crone in the little cottage will feed him;
her lovely daughter will soothe his gusty feet,
Another king offers him a piece of his kingdom;
old Merlin warns Death keeps tent ahead.

Night, and he sobs against an old oak
— terrible the guerdon of a hired killer.

MASTERPIECE

Every man is free
Be he in chains or at sea

Life is freedom
Its purpose liberty

Every man who has ever lived
     was meant to be
There is no device in fortune
There can be no simplicity in the egg
No chance no game no lottery bowl

WHAT CHANCE COMMAND?

Thunder! And my thunder! Out of the house, O God!
The infant hands that hang from a man,
the boyman face with immature smile
with never a day of dire pensivity
Hard hard rain! Raged the storm
in these French fields I'd a small olding body
heaving and sobbing vows never again to grip
the soul's household rail over which to puke
      the world's bad news
Overnight my hair will turn white
No chance for stone to peel even as an apple will
No mugger God to knock the elements dizzy
No speech that I sneak the miracle —

A DIFFERENCE OF ZOOS

I went to the Hotel Broog;
and it was there I imagined myself singing *Ave Maria*
      to a bunch of hoary ligneous Brownies.
I believe in gnomes, in midges;
I believe to convert the bogeyman,
take Medusa to Kenneth's;
beg Zeus Polyphemus a new eye;
and I thanked all the men who ever lived,
thanked life the world
      for the chimera, the gargoyle,
      the sphinx, the griffin,
      Rumpelstiltskin —
I sang *Ave Maria*
      for the Heap, for Groot,
      for the mugwump, for Thoth,
      the centaur, Pan;
I summoned them all to my room in the Broog,
the werewolf, the vampire, Frankenstein,
every monster imaginable
and sang and sang *Ave Maria* —
The room got to be unbearable!
I went to the zoo
and oh thank God the simple elephant.

BRECHT & BENN

His sons will be angels, or their sons,
       someday there will be angels —
But not then, then was the time of devils,
Hitler trying to outdo Kandinsky;
       he succeeded,
       he was the top Expressionist,
       no doubt about that —
And Benn, poor wretched Benn,
       running in and out of hospitals screaming:
"Nothing might be real at all!"

Evil with cunning, evil as duty, oh but to exploit it,
       bash it raw;
The dead adore the dead,
       and the living are compelling

Through the slumbering melancholy of Stalinallee
A flag and a dove flap a windy dirge;
I think of Ctesiphon's cranning harbor,
Ctesiphon where mantic poets stand knee-deep
       lifting handfuls of water.

SOME MOROCCAN WRITINGS

for Jane Bowles,
a brilliant lovely soul

ON ARAB LADIES' WEAR

Through the medina's winding lanes
in solemn biblical blue raiment
they speak belladonna eyes
a luminous language perhaps sanctified
        for sorrowing hearts

Stupid to call them nuns
to call liberty a bikini
Hollywood-beach paradise

Faces and bodies are nothing eternal
Clothed they honor its dying

ARAB MEN IN CAFES

Here no growling drunks
force sentiment in the company of men
here busy quiet and clear music pervade
Grouped together on hillsides
sipping mint tea and pipefuls of kief
the influences of dream and nature
are contiguous to this company of men

THE EUROPEAN SECTION IN TANGIER

By the benignity of its environ
this section of Europe and America
brings many similitudes to mind:
The plastic Abyssinian
     and the North Dakota gorilla girl
Predominate beastcries from Angleterre
     and the Congo sergeant's ineffectual despair
Nay, yet in the heart light of it
one culture must blend with another culture
(ancient Phrygia can tell)
to maintain the separation it demands

MAN ENTERING THE SEA, TANGIER

He walks into the summer-cold sea
arms folded
trying to keep the wave splashings
from further chilling him

He moves with hesitation
He'd rather not go in
But there he goes with a NOW IN
and becomes warm

That curious warm all too familiar
as when frogs from fish kicked
and fins winged flew
and whatever it was decided lungs
and a chance above the sea

He would it nothing more
than a holiday's dip
yet there he is
millions of years that are legs,
back into that biggest & strangest of wombs

Does he remember algae for skin
he
who calls the dinosaur his unfortunate brother?

And what with those sad anthropods on the shore
are they truly dead?
Drowned in air?

Life's entrance seemed easy
But death
that NOW OUT
There is some difficulty

AIR IS TO GO

Now he's against his own for.
For him the word is the way.
Yet there is no door.
Thus he saves all keys and compares them,
one is the same like the rest;
the rest are different like the one.
This one will open no door and let him in.
Inside he will receive words alien to thought.

He will seize space by his Arab-tap of shoulders,
he is the Evictor,
he seeks the Word, he
the tondrenched Dispossessor of Space-squatters
        has come to budge air.

SOME GREEK WRITINGS

for Bill Barker & Miss Portman

IN A WAY
the Greeks today
don't like the Acropolis
because
it hovers over them
as though mockingly
as though imprisoning them
in a you-can't-do-better-than-me
      abyss

No matter whicheverway
they look
that mark of history
      is impossible to miss

WHEN PRESIDENT EISENHOWER
came to Athens
he got a helicopter
and flew over the Acropolis
and looked down at it
      like only Zeus could

I told that to a sharp Englishman
who replied:
He's fortunate he did not fly over it
      like Icarus

PHAESTOS IS A VILLAGE WITH 25 FAMILIES

and one taverna
There my friend and I sat
drinking with the tallest Greek in the world
And though he must have been close to sixty
his face and body seemed those of a strong young prince
We could not speak each other's language
but drink after drink we talked about everything

And I learned by my little German
and my companion's little Greek
and the others their little French and English
"He shot twenty German officers"
"But he wouldn't shoot a soldier"
"He says they were young and good"
"Now that the war is over and no more officers
        he's unhappy"
"He's unhappy because the village has forgotten
        his heroics"
He sighed a sigh which seemed to say:
Those were the good old days
Having drunk so much I had to go to the toilet
and so did my friend and almost all the others
There was no toilet

Thus out into the pitch dark we staggered
behind the taverna we went
where
beneath the starriest sky I ever saw
we all did wondrously pee

ARES COMES AND GOES

Beside me, in all its martial pose,
        walks real opportunity.
Behind me the rose is all dried up,
and my beautiful loved one intoxicated.
I'm gonna follow my new friend to the end.

The snow falls ephemeral white;
we grey it, slush it;
we're off to render the world.
Join us, human promise.

Poor world, neglect as any star.
Whether a great collision is imminent
        or not
there's no going among pyramids to grieve.

Inherit of mankind
        we keep by candlelight;
something there is
        does not hold the world this night.
It's up to us;
        grass dies every step we take;
death's optimistic,
and yet it does imbibe us drive on.

He'd me carry his sword and shield;
I'd his helmet too,
but he says no
        says my posture's an embarrassment,

and takes back his weaponage to boot,
what a friend! I tell him so;
he doesn't care.
A thin ribsome horse appears;
he gets on it and . . . . .zoom!
      disappears.

THE DOUBLE AXE

Great Spirit, whose naughty child is Great Ego,
Two of one, whose elongated thanks share Providence,
Alas! Life's miseries many times frayed by joy;
Ulcerated by clown turned phantom,
Dragging behind bright colors, profound melancholy,
Ah twosome, cross a river;
The inhabitants, all covered with black moss,
Enkindle hopes with butterflies —

ACTIVE NIGHT

A tarsier bewrays the end of an epical rain
Burying beetles ponderously lug a dead rat
A moth, just a few seconds old, tumbles down fern
Bats are drinking flowers
The lonely tapir walks the river bottom
And up comes a manatee with a sea-anemone
        on its nose

AN EARLY DUTCH SCENE

The Dutch cartographer
small and round
sits on crude wood
stuffing his clay pipe

His jolly wife
carries a bundle of silver fish
They've a weaving daughter
whose lover corresponds from war
and an infant boy
who grabs the cat's whiskers

It is winter
and a fireplace
glows them cozy brown

A RACE OF SOUND

Sounds are running a race the trek the climb the swim
      the pace
And voices are edging up to roars and close behind
      the closing of doors the thump of rabbits
And coming up in the stretch the howling of ghosts
The humming of birds and now voices are neck and neck
With the climb of vines and the trek of penguins
The swim of fish is third and moving in the inside thunder
      and bombs and in the back stretch the thud of coffins
      the fall of timber the sway of palms
Voices are leading are leading heaving and breathing
      speaking and singing fully in the clear but hold hold
From out of nowhere the wail of cats the chomp of carrots
A squeaky shoe challenges for the lead Oh what a race!
Here comes the drop of a pin the cawk of a parrot
The breaking of glass the scratch of an itch
The crowds are going wild! yelling and kicking and jumping
— so wild they win the race

AFTER ANOTHER READING OF DANTE

There's a heavy sad humanness to hell,
But I cannot look on any living face
      and believe it sadder there.
I can find nothing human about heaven.

THERE CAN BE NO OTHER
APPLE FOR ME

In this lovely lonely orchard
perhaps stemmed for Eve's core
I move in applelight continuum
of no dimension no dominion

And all around are apples ripe for the picking
but I go for that out of reach one
and quite make it

1962

WRIT ON THE STEPS
OF PUERTO RICAN HARLEM

There's a truth limits man
A truth prevents his going any farther
The world is changing
The world *knows* it's changing
Heavy is the sorrow of the day
The old have the look of doom
The young mistake their fate in that look
This is truth
But it isn't *all* truth

Life has meaning
And I do not know the meaning
Even when I felt it were meaningless
I hoped and prayed and sought a meaning
It wasn't all frolic poesy
There were dues to pay
Summoning Death and God
I'd a wild dare to tackle Them
Death proved meaningless without Life
Yes the world is changing
But Death remains the same
It takes man away from Life
The only meaning he knows
And usually it is a sad business
This Death

I'd an innocence I'd a seriousness
I'd a humor save me from amateur philosophy
I am able to contradict my beliefs

I am able able
Because I want to know the meaning of everything
Yet sit I like a brokenness
Moaning: Oh what responsibility
I put on thee Gregory
Death and God
Hard hard it's hard

I learned life were no dream
I learned truth deceived
Man is not God
Life is a century
Death an instant

LOGOS LOGOS LOGOS

Alas, but it doth seem
Language cannot break the
WHAT WHEN HOW WHY barrier —
God Gott Godh Guth
What was before the sun?
In the beginning was the word
Why?
Because why's the end of Broadway, that's why
Enigmatic lies don't help much —
There's a sturdy etymological staff
Whose scientific and poetic investigations
Into the source of Zend
Leads nowhere —

I summon an altongue, a noumenal rune,
Nosce te ipsum, a campanology
To guide me in my hackuring
This uranic whorl
I don't care the result
A toothwort on the salver will do —
The center is everywhere
Yet there be an abaxial center
There where the aardwolf chews on the banderole;
A rag to cerement the world —

Alas, when I think to forget
Language, I go out —
At heart, in the company of people,
The sky is seldom and chance;
Crowded bars or tiny rooms
They drink they talk they dance;
It was like that last Sunday;
There's not enough time —
A bee's both honey and sting;
My aceldama unirama screaming Loki hammer
Basta

SOUL

Whose origin was devised by man
Whose source no anatomy chart can unradiate
Busy are the secretaries of the sun
Who depict it a secret fire that cannot smoke
A swimless star harboring vital yet invisible
Mighty yet ever in danger

The soul has an innermost failing
       when the mind wages a crisis
It is the body that moves in totality
       to the fix of entrance and departure
All else divisions be the mind's routine

Oh but can it be a white heart made of air?

GROWING PAINS

What scarce given measure finger-runs
across this noughtsome face?
What desperate inch to flay?
What beauty to spoor?

A bird on a branch
watches
the sun avalanche.

A CITY CHILD'S DAY

for Mr. Mason & son

No rooster wakes a child's city day
More likely an alarm clock
Yet whatever occasions it hail the dawn
Out into it he goes
Hands in pockets carefree and with glee
The gutter is his pastoral path
The fire hydrant his favorite toy
The pavement he walks covers perhaps
A trail that goes way back to a time of trees
When trees were plentiful when birds and beasts
When streams flowed and hills were visible
When Redmen lightly strode
And Dutchmen wore buckled hats and shoes
— Ah this walk is not new it is old
Ancient as the earth it covers
And older it grows

Grownups do not go where children go
At break of day their worlds split apart
Quite often it is night blends them
And even then sleep distinguishes them
Empty lots and stoops
Here the society of children gather
Boys may join the girls; most don't, yet he'd rather
They adorn and garland him he is their champion
He'll lead them to hopscotch and chalk writing
And awearied he'll sit with the fairest of them all
She with the regnant air of a queen will look away
As does he, like a proud Viking, from the writing on the wall

Fire is not fire but a magnificent truck
A shiny bell and uniformed men whose hats yell
With excitement and all that is wonderful
Away they siren even when the lights aren't green

Late noon falls like a heavy bassoon
Grownups pass by like sleepy shadows
No sound no word
And the big lady in the window, who is she?
She's carroty fingers and breadloaf arms!
Into alcneness he leaps and frightens a cat

O rare alley cat
Ever-bruised tom and ever-pregnant feline
Once so familiar and now in decline
No longer do you cuddle under parked cars
Climb in and out broken windows
And on fences meow to the stars

He runs he stops he kicks a can
He skips and over a hydrant he hops
It's time for the big boys to gather and play
He hurries he runs he knows the way
Just in time! they're choosing sides
They won't choose him he's still too small
Alone again
He runs he stops he picks up a stick
And floats it down a street running water
While his heart so like a clock
Tells him his day will soon be over

His exhaustion is lashed in crucifixional poses
Against buildings against cars against people
The day is changing the day is always changing
What happens to it when he goes home?
He's changing too
By why oh why does he feel for the worse?
What good the day if he's not good in it?
Left behind, demoted from his time,
He's unable to adhibit and nightcap his day
The Beginning remains unknown
The End remains unknown
This is his great sorrow
Day is all he knows
Not Night

THEY

They, that unnamed "they,"
they've knocked me down
      but I got up
I always get up —
And I swear when I went down
      quite often I took the fall;
nothing moves a mountain but itself —
They, I've long ago named them me.

WRIT IN HORACE GREELEY SQUARE

I know I'm one who
        even if he does see the light
still won't be completely all right
        and good for that

Yesterday I believed in man today I don't
        and tomorrow
           tomorrow's a toss-up

Somedays I see all people
        in deep pain with life
And other days
        I see them victors
living things great as to question their living

To see back and forth like that and not go crazy
        is something
Something Miss Brody ran home to jump out of
Contradiction, that good virtue,
        could prevent many a silly death

Or was it a hilarious death
the prodigal son arrives home
        "Hello pa"
        and jumps out the window

Out the window
Oh out the window is an image of man disrupts
        the image I would of him
A block away is that high diveboard
How many dove from there?
I clearly recall a huge ape dropping down

And you, Mr. Greeley, what say you
        in all your bronze watchings?
What newspaper now?
Tells it man is in deep pain with life?
Man is the victory of life?

P.S. 42

When I think back to grammar school
I am overcome with breathlessness and sweet feeling —
Freighted to that glorious mahogany time
when bluecoats cheered each other with pewter mugs
and snow-hunched sentries eyed young Washington dismount
and Indians covered their horses with Algonquin rugs
Where perhaps a goodly witch buying sassafras
rubbed shoulders with Ben Franklin picking
        half-pennies from a tiny purse —

I played Christopher Columbus aged ten
in the great assembly hall before all
and I clearly remember as I sat
dreamily on the docks of Genoa
the beautiful picture of Washington at Valley Forge
Quite disastrous that
because when Queen Isabella asked my name
I said George

I learned in grammar school
that Lincoln walked many miles for a book
which he read lying on his stomach
            before a bubbling-kettle fireplace
That's how I wanted to read a book!
So as soon as the class was over
I hurried a mile from my neighborhood library
            to another library
Of course they wouldn't issue me a card
"Use the library in your own neighborhood"
So I stole my book
and late that night
under my blanket with a little flashlight
I read
And I do not exaggerate when I say
I fully felt the joy that was Lincoln's

It was the fourth grade when the teacher
took us to Trinity Church to see
Alexander Hamilton's grave —
Carmine wanted to laugh
The way he laughed made me laugh
And the way we laughed made the whole class laugh
He did that at the Planetarium
and because of it the teacher denied us the stars
When I was young I was able to be serious if I wanted
I did not laugh
He made funny faces
            scratched himself in dirty places
He did his utmost to deny me Hamilton
With all my might I listened to what the teacher
had to say about a man whose life I hold in high esteem

I never cared much about Patrick Henry
and Paul Revere too
Nor was there anything about the redcoats I liked
They were the enemy
no different from the Germans and the Japs
       I was a year later taught to hate
Yet one redcoat there was
       made me see the majesty of the English
It was the death of General Wolfe
the biggest picture in the school
The battle was in full force
war at its loveliest
and he lay there
       dying in the arms of soldiers

I'd a D conduct in that school
Never the tack on the teacher's chair
but oh, I was bad when I was bad

FOR THOSE WHO COMMIT SUICIDE

It were better to be alive in a world of death
than to be dead in a world of life;

they kill themselves because they fear death;

only the lovers of life are fit to die —

FOR —

What stinking beady wart
      like a ten ton toad
squats on life's sick nose
        puffing molten mega-pus
ever ready to hop upon the earth
        and splash all over us

The bomb's a decoy
I've seen the horror of narcotics
      eat the day
They were all sad
sad mainly because life was insufficient
They were sickly sad
And drugs were a filthy nurse

DANGER

Because of me narcotics are —
Useless you enforcers of safety
scheming ways and hows to keep out of me;
there is no out, there is only in,
and you are all in danger —

Useless to deface the world with:
Beware, Do Not Trespass, Skullcrossbones,
E Pericoloso Sporgersi —
My property is sorrow!
No fence
No warning there —

AFTER READING "IN THE CLEARING"

for the author, Robert Frost

Old bard I like you more
        now that I know you're
        no Saturday Evening Post philosopher
Nay but such who plagiarizes God
Whose pen is a rod
        miracling all that is lovely old lovely bard

I would not like to think
        what's safe is safer done
        that it were an ill-planned link
        you and Washington
A poet can be a true friend
        upon which a politician could depend
Yet as history doth show
        out of power no poems grow
Such twinship ends up
        with the poet in the cup
Were you younger this were so
        but you are old old you are Rome
        the wisdom of time — and no crow
        maketh your snowy head its home

Poe is my only American poet, sir
And my homeland were Greece and England
Shelley is my ichor — Demeter is my mother
And of the living Ginsberg's metaphor
        is all I care to understand
You undoubtedly think unwell of us
But we are your natural children

THE PLIGHT OF IACCHUS

His mother was the mother of earth;
when she walked trees bowed,
rocks relented,
and shepherds celebrated
— and Core, his sister,
had Death his brother-in-law.

FLIGHT

School girls in blue frocks
       led by benign nuns
— overhead, jet streams

How miraculous the B-52
sleek orange and silver
       long as blue

My youth's heart loved
       the P-38
the doves of war

I'd a Comet from Paris
       to Athens
Alexander! what leap
       from thy phalanx

SECOND NIGHT IN N.Y.C. AFTER 3 YEARS

I was happy I was bubbly drunk
The street was dark
I waved to a young policeman
He smiled
I went up to him and like a flood of gold
Told him all about my prison youth
About how noble and great the convicts were
And about how I just returned from Europe
Which wasn't half as enlightening as prison
And he listened attentively I told no lie
Everything was truth and humor
He laughed
He laughed
And it made me so happy I said:
"Absolve it all, kiss me!"
"No no no no!" he said
      and hurried away.

AZEGBEQUX

The astronaut was a Fulbright
A student of Italian painting
And when everything was GO
Up was not Tiepolo

WRIT ON THE EVE OF MY 32nd BIRTHDAY

a slow thoughtful spontaneous poem

I am 32 years old
and finally I look my age, if not more.
Is it a good face what's no more a boy's face?
It seems fatter. And my hair,
it's stopped being curly. Is my nose big?
The lips are the same.
And the eyes, ah the eyes get better all the time.
32 and no wife, no baby; no baby hurts,
        but there's lots of time.
I don't act silly any more.
And because of it I have to hear from so-called friends:
"You've changed. You used to be so crazy so great."
They are not comfortable with me when I'm serious.
Let them go to the Radio City Music Hall.
- 32; saw all of Europe, met millions of people;
        was great for some, terrible for others.
I remember my 31st year when I cried:
"To think I may have to go another 31 years!"
I don't feel that way this birthday.
I feel I want to be wise with white hair in a tall library
        in a deep chair by a fireplace.
Another year in which I stole nothing.
8 years now and haven't stole a thing!
I stopped stealing!
But I still lie at times,
and still am shameless yet ashamed when it comes
        to asking for money.

32 years old and four hard real funny sad bad wonderful
        books of poetry
— the world owes me a million dollars.

I think I had a pretty weird 32 years.
And it weren't up to me, none of it.
No choice of two roads; if there were,
        I don't doubt I'd have chosen both.
I like to think *chance* had it I play the bell.
The clue, perhaps, is in my unabashed declaration:
"I'm good example there's such a thing as called soul."
I love poetry because it makes me love
        and presents me life.
And of all the fires that die in me,
there's one burns like the sun;
it might not make day my personal life,
        my association with people,
        or my behavior toward society,
but it does tell me my soul has a shadow.

New Directions Paperbooks—A Partial Listing

For complete listing request free catalog from
New Directions, 80 Eighth Avenue, New York 10011

†Bilingual

For complete listing request free catalog from
New Directions, 80 Eighth Avenue, New York 10011

†Bilingual